T0120711

WHAT GOD HAS JOINED TOGETHER

A CHASTISING RELATIONSHIP

LARRY ADAMS ED D

WESTBOW
PRESS®
A DIVISION OF THOMAS NELSON
& ZONDERVAN

WestBow Press books may be ordered through booksellers or by contacting:

WestBow Press
A Division of Thomas Nelson & Zondervan
1663 Liberty Drive
Bloomington, IN 47403
www.westbowpress.com
844-714-3454

All scripture quotations are taken from the
King James Version. Public domain.

ISBN: 978-1-6642-9906-1 (sc)
ISBN: 978-1-6642-9907-8 (e)

Library of Congress Control Number: 2023908060

Print information available on the last page.

WestBow Press rev. date: 05/04/2023

Table Of Contents

Foreword

When I think about relationships and how God has joined them together for his purpose in the beginning. I realize the need for understanding how important it is for God to guide us through that understanding. To know that we have no control over our lives without him. Understanding that life is not about our feelings, our needs, our imaginations or our perceptions, but on the purpose of our Creator. It is an opportunity to fill God's purpose. What God has joined together in a relationship is more than we can perceive. It involves obedience, responsibility, spirituality and faith. God has joined together everything we need for a successful relationship. In fact, what God has joined together will include himself.

In this book, I attempt to re-examine relationships in light of scripture for the purpose of revealing some misunderstood truth about relationships. I hope to provide the reader with a view of relationship in light of how God would have us view it from a spiritual perspective. A relationship is the process of becoming one with each other. It cannot be done by man alone even as a world view. A healthy relationship is a spiritual relationship. We need to look deeper into the word of God for understanding what God has joined together. Scripture states *"what God has joined together let no man put asunder"* (Mark 10:9, kjv)

In our society today we want to take what God has created and make it work our way. When it comes to a relationship we selfishly replace that responsibility with our personal desires. We are expecting the relationship to work under our control and understanding, giving no thought to the fact that we really have no foundation for that relationship to stand. Even in considering the things that are most valuable to us in a relationship, the appearance, personality, character, money, sex or even intelligence are not foundations for a relationship. They may be valuable to us but not enough to base our lives on. They are not even stable themselves because nothing stays the same but God. When we have our own values and put them in the place of righteousness we will never be able to see or understand the truth. Our feelings and our values combined are a deadly combination for making decisions morally or ethically if not guided by the principles of God. Therefore, in a relationship we should consider a required commitment with the understanding of what that means spiritually and physically. A relationship must be about oneness and with love. In order to understand a relationship we need to understand God's will for our lives.

Acknowledgments

I thank God for His Holy Spirit and for my Lord and Savior Jesus Christ who has blessed my life in so many ways and has allowed me the opportunity to praise Him for who He is.

My primary thanks go to my church family, my former Pastor Dr A. L. Hamilton Sr and my present Pastor Landis Fisher. The inspiration of God's word has gracefully guided my life as I press toward the mark of the high calling of God in Jesus Christ. I also want to thank God for blessing me with a wonderful wife Julia who has demonstrated love and trust that is beyond measure. An example of what God has joined together in the simple obedience of the word of God.

Introduction

Man's view of joining together often carries with it a standard of how that process should please him. The purpose of that joining has to be personal or at least adjustable. Man is limited in his understanding of how to join anything that requires perception and purpose. And he must rely on God to see the whole picture. What God our Creator has joined together is completed because God is understanding. (Proverb 8:14, kjv) And the purpose of this joining is oneness, first with God and then with man.

Man is liable for his joining in every area of his life. For scripture tells us that we should *"not be unequally yoked together with unbelievers; for what fellowship hath righteousness with unrighteousness? And what communion hath light with darkness?" (I Corinthians 6:14, kjv)* God never told Adam to go and find him a wife she was never loss. She would be found in the Lord. God still gives husbands and wives. However, we decide to exercise our view of an acceptable mate. Not only in this type of relationship but many of our associate choices in life. Who can know what is best for us than God that will serve His purpose? Let us be reminded to *"first seek you the kingdom of God and His righteousness and all these other things will be added." (Matthew 6:33, kjv)* And finally, the Lord has made clear In His word that we should forsake not the assembly together of ourselves. (Hebrew 10:25, kjv)

There is no doubt in my mind that the number one problem in the world today is relationship. It has become a number one struggle in our society. We have taken it for the most part lightly and assuming that it doesn't really matter or simply charged it to our attitudes or our knowledge. We have always sought a relationship in our own way based on what we either have been taught or advised. Naturally we want to have control and choice about that relationship or we don't accept it. And based on our environment and influence from the world we allow our relationship to be governed. Not realizing due to a lack of knowledge it would ever occur to us naturally that there is more to a relationship than we actually understand. Our perception of a relationship only reveals what appears to be the meaning and method of a true relationship. By and large deeper issues will arise out of these perspectives. The quality and expectations of that relationship will be tested to the strength of its foundation to satisfy that relationship. The results will easily expose itself to the truth and purpose of a relationship. In other words God's purpose is to be one with him in love. If not this, your relationship has no ground to stand on and will fail. Remember it was God who instituted relationship.

Dedication

I dedicate this book and pray that hearts will be touched In the name of our Lord and Savior Jesus Christ. To the faithful ministers and counselors who stand fast on the word of God and proclaim the authority of the word; which is the hope of healing the wounded souls and changing lives in the name of Jesus Christ.

Now I beseech you, brethren, by the name of our Lord Jesus Christ, that you speak the same thing, and that there be no divisions among you, but that ye be perfectly joined together in the same mind and in the same judgment.

— I Corinthians 1:10 KJV

Chapter 1

WHAT GOD HAS JOINED TOGETHER

I n the first dispensation God created man in his own image, in the image of God created he him; male and female created he them. (Genesis 1:27, kjv) This image was a personal, rational, and moral being. Man was crowned with glory and honor (Psalms 8:58, kjv) but subject to God his creator. (Genesis 2:15-17, kjv) Sin entered the world and man became separated from God. (Genesis 3:8-10, kjv) The purpose of God is oneness as taught in the bible. (John 17:21, kjv) The divine intention and purpose of God is that He would have fellowship with man as in obedience. A dispensation is a period during of which man is being tested by God in respect to his obedience to some specific revelation of the will of God.

The purpose of each dispensation is to place man under a specific rule of conduct that would correspond to God's specific plan of fellowship. What God was joining together was an image and likeness of himself spiritually. Man is a tri-unity, a makeup of body, soul and spirit, a tripartite nature. (1 Thessalonians 5:23, kjv) But God is Spirit. (John 4:24, kjv) God blessed man and after providing him a wife He specifically commanded them to be fruitful and multiply and fill the earth. (Genesis 1:28, kjv) And as all the other things God had made said it was good. The first institution joined together by

God was the marriage of man and woman. What God had joined together He expect to keep together. First of all, obedience was required as the foundational strength to stay together. They were taught to be responsible for all that God had given them dominion over in the earth but because of sin, man voluntarily separated himself from God in disobedience not realizing what the effect that sin would have on future generations to come. What God had joined together was a <u>spiritual relationship</u> between himself and *man.* *"According as he has chosen us in him before the foundation of the world, that we should be holy and without blame before him, in love." (Ephesians 1:4, kjv)* Because of the fall of man redemption is required to restore man to his relationship with God. Man is no longer innocent. The stewardship of innocence ended in judgment in the expulsion from Eden. (Genesis 3:24, kjv)

At this point we realize that as sin had entered the world <u>deception</u> would follow. This would not stop God's plan and purpose for man which was to be fruitful and multiply and fill the earth. God has given man everything he needs to fill his purpose if guided by Him. God joined grace, faith and obedience as a wonderful plan of salvation. There was always order in the way that God dealt with His creation. For instance as God joined Adam and Eve together they were as one, the first institution established by God on earth. God has demonstrated all the time that He wanted oneness with mankind as oneness in a relationship. We can learn a lot from God through His grace, faith and the importance of <u>obedience</u>. Starting with the grace and favor with God they both were of course equally yoke *as in God's word. "Be ye not unequally yoked together with unbelievers;*

for what fellowship hath righteousness with unrighteousness?" (11 Corinthians 6:14, kjv) As a divine requirement for marriage this is an acceptable guide to a rightful oneness in a marriage. <u>Obedience</u> is better than sacrifice and we do want to please God as He wants the best for us. The two are one spirit in God and His purpose for them. The world has changed since that time but God will never change. (Malachi 3:6, kjv) God still requires a faith based life from all mankind. Because whatsoever is not of faith is sin. (Romans 14:23, kjv) God does not join us with sin and call it matrimony.

As the prophet Jeremiah says *"let us join ourselves to the Lord in a perpetual covenant that shall not be forgotten." (Jeremiah 50:5, kjv) Remember that he that* is joined to the Lord is one spirit. (I Corinthians 6:17, kjv) It is important that this generation be reminded that ever since Cain slew Abel we were introduced to *spiritual warfare* and *rebellion*. We are still in that warfare. (Ephesians 6:12, kjv) Despite the fact, we know we can depend on God to help us to live faithfully. For *He says in his word that "no weapon formed against thee shall prosper". (Isaiah 54:17, kjv)* We are always in the presence of God and He is always in control. God only joins and puts together that which is holy and righteous. Make no mistake about it, what God has joined together is a requirement to complete His plans for mankind and to demonstrate His love.

What, therefore, God hath joined together, let not man put asunder.

— Mark 10:9

Chapter II

MAN AND WOMAN
IN MARRIAGE

I n thinking about relationships, what it means, and how God meant for it to be in terms of creation, we have to think about what God has joined together. Even though there is a lot to assume about the subject of relationships when it comes to man and woman. I wonder what God really had in mind when He instituted a relationship as a part of creation between a man and a woman. Scripture clearly states that as far as God is concerned He views them as "one". This seems to me to be the definition or purpose of what God has joined together, "oneness" between a man and a woman. After all God did say in His word "*it is not good that the man should be alone; I will make him an help fit for him*". *(Genesis 2:18, kjv)* Truly, in the unity of the God head there was a distinct but binding relationship. As far as marriage is concerned, our definition and perception of relationships today has taken a different worldview, value and purpose. We seemed to have loss the understanding and respect for what God's purpose is for a relationship in marriage. Men have struggled with the understanding of relationships since the fall of man. And since that time men have not considered the foundation for which the relationship must stand. They selfishly bind themselves together in unity that has no real purpose or substantial foundation. They refuse to be guided by the creator who instituted marriage and depending on their feelings, selfishness and persuasive desires. A relationship is suppose to be a process of becoming one with each other. A healthy relationship is a spiritual relationship. But because of man's view and definition of a relationship, it has become strictly physical and that imposes a problem.

What God has joined together with love, faith and grace is a successful relationship that can be depended upon as a strong foundation of unity in a marriage. What God has joined together is a spiritual blessing and carries with it the power of the Holy Spirit of hope. Men and women need to understand what God has joined together and its purpose. We cannot allow our relationships to be based on selfishness and no oneness. For the scriptures says *"can two walk together accept they agree" (Amos 3:3, kjv)* selfishness does not seek oneness with another. There cannot be a relationship interpersonal or otherwise without a correct foundation for which the purpose of that relationship can stand. That relationship must first be with God and in love. (I Corinthians 13:3-5, kjv) We are born in iniquity and it is our natural desire to please self. (Psalms 51:5, Ephesians 2, kjv) Remember oneness is the goal and strength of our relationship. Oneness with another has no self, only love that binds it together and fulfills the purpose for which God intended.

In understanding what God has joined together includes a spiritual commitment. Meaning that this connection should not be based on emotions or physical feelings. What God has joined together is not natural but spiritual. This is why God says *"let not man put asunder". (Mark 10:19, kjv)* Man cannot separate that which is spiritual from God. I call your attention to the conception and birth of Jesus. *"Before they came together, Mary was found with child of the Holy Spirit. Joseph was minded to put her away privately but an angel of the Lord appeared to him in a dream, saying, Joseph, that which is conceived in her is of the Holy Spirit. (This was joined together by the Lord God) (Matthew 1:21, kjv)* This was God's anointed and the fulfillment of God's promise. *"And she shall bring forth a son, and thou shalt call his name"* Jesus, for he shall save his people from their sins"*. (Matthew 1:21, kjv)* Everything that God joins together is not greater than a miracle.

God still joins relationships together to fulfill His purpose. Not only people who want to be married but those who want to have relationship with Him. As a matter of fact, He invites mankind to come to Him. (Matthew 11:28, kjv) But it has to be on His terms to fill his purpose. God only joins together in holiness especially in His spirit.

What God has joined together will result in godliness, holiness and righteousness. Considering a statement made by Jesus himself that *"I am not sent but unto the lost sheep of the house of Israel". (Matthew 15:24, kjv)* These are of the Jews, the covenant people of the Lord. As God has joined together the covenant people the Jews, He commanded *"behold, I send the promise of my Father upon you, but tarry ye in the city of Jerusalem, until ye be endued with the power from on high." (Luke 24:49, kjv)* Surely these were God's chosen people that God has joined to himself with compassion and mission to. (Matthew 15:24, kjv)

We as God's children can play a big part in what God has join together if we obey His command to *"Be ye not unequally yoked together with unbelievers; for what fellowship hath righteousness with unrighteousness? And what communion hath light with darkness? (II Corinthians 6:14, kjv)*

What, therefore, God hath joined together, let not man put asunder.

— Mark 10:9

Chapter III

CHRIST AND THE CHURCH

God the Father had planned the Church according to scripture "Blessed be the God and Father of our Lord Jesus Christ, who hath blessed us with all spiritual blessings in heavenly places in Christ. (Ephesians 1:3, kjv) Our blessings are a declaration but His blessings are deeds. God has blessed us in heavenly places in Christ with all spiritual blessings. This does not say that we are <u>with Christ</u> but that we are <u>in Christ</u>. God has joined us who are believers to His son in the heaven. In planning the Church God chose us in Christ, He predestine us to the place of son ship and He made us accepted in the Beloved. All of this because of His divine will. God the Father planned the Church, God the Son paid for the Church, and God the Holy Spirit protects the Church. God carries our mind back to eternity past to make us realize that salvation is altogether of God and whatsoever God has joined together let no man put asunder. God's purpose will prevail. He brings us to the place of faith in Christ and to a saving knowledge of the grace of God that is revealed in the Lord Jesus Christ.

Scripture states that *"if children, then heirs- heirs of God, and joint heirs with Christ – if so be that we suffer with him, that we may be also glorified together. (Romans 8:17, kjv)* For as many as are led by the Spirit of God, they are the sons of God.

(Romans 8:14, kjv) God chose Israel in time; He chose the Church in eternity. God did this connection for a purpose: *"that we should be holy and without blamed before him in love". (Ephesians 1:4, kjv)* God chose us in order that He might sanctify us. Now that God has made us to be a part of the Church (the called out ones) we have the right to enjoy His blessings and glorify His name. We understand that election is God's choosing us in Christ. It is all because of His mercy. The free will of man is never violated because of the election of God. The man who is lost makes his own choice. Without free will in the grace of God, how can He save the world?

God the son paid the price for the Church. (Ephesians 1:7, kjv) The plans of God the Father have been placed in the hands of Christ, who is moving into time and space to build the Church.

In His building He redeemed us by the shedding of His blood. We cannot over emphasize this as a fact. Redemption is the primary work of Christ. "In whom we have the redemption." This is the reason Christ came to earth. To give His life as a ransom for many. (Matthew 20:28, kjv) *"Without the shedding of blood is no remission."* (Hebrew 9:22, kjv) Forgiveness depends on the shedding of blood. It depends and demands payment of the penalty for sin. God cannot forgive until the penalty has been paid. This is the only way we can have forgiveness for our sins. Christ bought the Church with his own blood and paid the penalty for our sins according to the riches of His grace. Look what God has joined together. *HE bought us in order to set us free!*

But "in the fullness of time", what is this "fullness of time?" The "pleroma" is when everything is bought under the relationship of Jesus Christ. This is the mystery that is revealed to us that is in the dispensation of the fullness of times when he will gather together in one all things in Christ. Here God will put all thing under his feet. (Hebrew 2:8, kjv) The Son, Jesus Christ on behalf of the Church will reward us with an inheritance. (Ephesians 1:11-12, kjv) It is the overall purpose and plan of God that believers should have a part in Christ inheritance. Can we imagine everything belonging to you? That is, what God has made. If Christ belongs to you everything is yours even death. God has predestined this to the saved. This is not out of our merit but out of His grace. The Church is very important to God. It is a part of God's great plan for man. When we look at the work of the Holy Spirit we see how He regenerates us, how He is a refuge for us and how He gives reality to our lives by regeneration. (Ephesians 1:13, kjv) By accepting God's work <u>for us</u> to the work of the Holy Spirit <u>in us</u> is the work of the Church.

"For above all principality, and power and might, and dominion, and every name that is named, not only in this world, also in that which is to come; And hath put all things under his feet, and gave him to be the head overall things to the church which is his body, the fullness of him that filleth all in all. (Ephesians 1:21-23, kjv) The true believers born again and washed in His blood. The Church is the temple of God so is your body. (I Corinthians 3:16–17, kjv)

Chapter IV

GOD AND HIS COVENANT PEOPLE

The ancient world as well as the modern world is filled with treaties or covenants with groups of people, organizations and often as military alliances. This analogy is used to describe God's entering into a relationship with His people. In referring to the covenants that God made with His people, first the Noahic Covenant after the flood, God promised not to destroy the earth again. (Genesis 9:9-17, kjv) In the Abrahamic

Covenant (Genesis 15:18, 17:1-19, kjv), God promised to make his name great as well as a nation. Terms were established by both these covenants by God who vowed them. The covenant at Mount Sinai was also set in place in terms of God's law where He calls upon the Israelite to agree upon these terms. (Exodus 24:1-8, kjv) This would make them His covenant people as they promised to obey his revealed laws. This was the beginning of the fifth dispensation being the law. The people acknowledged the covenant as they worshiped. This is what God has so gracefully joined together with the conditions of obedience. We must also notice that God lives among his people in *"Ark of the Covenant"* (Numbers 10:38, kjv) as a personal dwelling place. The fact that God makes a promise to have a descendant of David on the throne is also a "Covenant" (II Samuel 23:5; 2 Chronicles 13:5; 21:7, kjv)

Despite all the effort God has made they broke His covenant again and again to the point where the bible says that God promises to make a new covenant with his people. (Jeremiah 31:31–34, kjv) Because of His incredible grace He gave them a covenant they will not break, because He would forgive them for their sins and iniquities. This was because of the blood of Christ. (Luke 22:20; Hebrews 8:8; 9:15; 12:28, kjv) Jesus was the mediator of the new covenant. (Hebrews 8:6; 12:24, kjv) His blood was the *"blood of the new Covenant".* (Luke 22:20; I Corinthians 11:25, kjv) The writer to Hebrews as well as Paul demonstrate different ways in which this Covenant is superior to the old covenant in that it has better promises and its glory will be to God. A Covenant between human beings (Genesis 21:27, 32; Joshua 9:11, 15, kjv) or between God and His people (Exodus 34:10; Deuteronomy

4:23, kjv) often require a pledge of "Covenant loyalty". A permanent record was also kept in the temple of this. One of the purposes of these Covenants was mutual protection in war and peace. In today's case, spiritual warfare. (Genesis 26:28-29, 31:50-52 kjv) (Joshua 9:15-16, II Kings 17:41, kjv)

Special illustration to God's Covenant people is the marriage contract. *"Because the Lord has been a witness between you and the wife of your youth. She is your companion and your wife by Covenant. (Mark 2:14, kjv)* And as far man is concerned, God says, behold, I establish my Covenant with you with your descendants after you. (Genesis 9:9-11, kjv) Don't forget at one time you were without Christ, being aliens from the commonwealth of Israel and strangers from the Covenants of promise, having no hope and without God in the world. Ephesians 2:12, kjv) But now the Jews are united and determined to serve God. (II Kings 11:17, II Chronicles 15:12, Nehemiah 10:29, kjv) As the result of the Covenants of God, let us realize that a sacrifice has been made. As the scripture teaches, obedience is better the sacrifice, by the same token God's will is better than obedience. (Matthew 5:23-24, kjv) Covenants are protected and insured by God according to His will. Biblical Covenants do not represent anything new in the world. Israel used these methods in their worship, renewing regularly the Covenant relationship with God. Johnathan acknowledged David's right to the throne. (I Samuel 18:3, 23:18, kjv) An agreement that was "a Covenant of the Lord" meant that the Lord was its witness and guarantee. (Samuel 20:8, kjv) King Zedekiah made a Covenant with the people of Jerusalem, releasing the Hebrews from slavery. (Jeremiah 34:8, kjv)

In the history of Israel they had

often made Covenant agreements with foreigners despite God's warning. (Joshua 9; Judges 2:2, kjv) In the book of Isaiah, he spoke of a "Covenant of death" political leaders had made. (Isaiah 28:15, kjv) They thought they had purchased a Covenant of protection from their enemies. But the prophets had reminded them that there was no security against God's judgment. That it was no more than a ritual to a foreign god of death. God's Covenant with His people was God's grace in relating to His people by initializing His Covenant with them. Noah received God's first Covenant. (Genesis 9:9, 17, kjv) This was a divine oath or promise from God not to repeat the flood. This Covenant called for no response from human beings it was solely a promise and oath from God. In Genesis 6 God had already confirmed a Covenant already established. God's first Covenant protects human life and animals from destruction. This priority of protection of life remains the foundation of God's relationship with His people. God's second Covenant with Abraham involved a man of faith. (Genesis 15:6, kjv) Understand that this was not a Covenant that was earned by good works but rather could be directed by God's actions and His purpose. It involved divine promises not human obedience.

In the process of redemption from Egyptian slavery, Israel found itself in God's Covenant as His people. The situation was not based on an affirmation of human faithfulness or righteousness, but the confession of God's salvation. (Exodus 9:4, kjv) The promise did not come from God but from the people. *"They were to obey my voice indeed, and keep my Covenant". Then they would become a "Kingdom of priest, an holy nation."* (Exodus 6:5-6, kjv) The people had accepted this responsibility as was read from the "book of the Covenant" and "the blood of the Covenant" as the blood was sprinkled on the altar and on the people. (Exodus 24:3-8, kjv) God included with this Covenant the Sabbath Covenant to identify themselves as God's Covenant people "Lord God made a Covenant with us in Horeb". *"The Lord made not this Covenant with our fathers, but with us, even us, who are all of us here alive this day." (Deuteronomy 5:2-3, kjv)* A major element of blessing is that God will make His Covenant stand for His people. (Leviticus 20:9, kjv) God's Covenants are never selfish demands of a victorious, powerful overlord placing unreasonable demands on its subject. God works in favor of His Covenant people. Remember God gave us a Covenant not a compromise.

God's Covenant to His people characterized Him and distinguished

Him from the other gods of the nations in that He was the one "who keepeth Covenant and mercy with the servants that walk before thee with all their hearts." (I Kings 8:23; II Chronicles 6:14; Hebrews 1:5; 9:32, kjv) Although throughout history God's people were not always faithful to the Covenant. An example was David's son King Solomon who set out to breaking the Covenant, worshiping other gods and demonstrating a model Israel consistent to their history forgetting the Covenant. (Proverb 2:17, kjv) The Covenant relationship becomes so characteristic that the Psalmist in worship and wisdom teaching reminded Israel to remember God and His Covenant. It then was the keeping of the Covenant that led to mercy and truth. (Psalms 25:10; 103:18, kjv) God's Covenant has a future. If Israel appointed would not be God's servant to fulfill the Gentile mission,

God will raise up a servant who will be a "light to the Gentiles". Forgiveness would characterize God's relationship to the new Covenant people. (Jeremiah 33:19-26, kjv) The new word for Covenant is the "New Testament" which follows the Septuagint, the earliest Greek translation of the Hebrew "berith" or Covenant. God has joined together mercy for His Covenant people.

Now I beseech you, brethren, by the name of our Lord Jesus Christ, that you speak the same thing, and that there be no divisions among you, but that ye be perfectly joined together in the same mind and in the same judgment.

— I Corinthians 1:10 KJV

Chapter V

BAPTISM AND SALVATION

Baptism that involves the immersion or dipping of a believer in Christ in water symbolizes the complete renewal and change in the believer's life. Also testifying to and sharing, the death, burial, and resurrection of Jesus Christ as a public confession of salvation. As with most Christian practices and beliefs, the background of baptism with water lies in practice of the Jewish community. The word *"baptizo"* meaning to immerse, dip, or submerge" is used metaphorically in

Isaiah 21:4 to mean, "go down, (perish)" and in II Kings 5:14 as with Naaman's dipping in the Jordan River seven times for cleansing from his disease. The emerging carries with it the emphasis on purity as the result of a resurrection and newness of life. At one time a heavy emphasis was put on ritual washing to cleanse from impurity. Even the priest were required to bathe prior to offering sacrifices. (Leviticus 16:4, 24, kjv) John the Baptist immersed those sinners who repented and had a change of mind and heart. (John 1:6, 11, kjv) What was required was repentance, confession, evidence of change of lives, and the understanding and the belief that the coming Messiah would baptize with the Holy Spirit. (Matthew 3:11, kjv) John was preparing a community for God's great salvation. This was along with the fact that John baptized Jesus that was to fulfill all righteousness. (Matthew 3:15, kjv)

Jesus himself did not do water baptism his disciples did. (John 4:1-2, kjv) Reason is, when Jesus comes into a life, the Holy Spirit comes also and with His presence purifies. He empowers and cleanses the believer with a spiritual baptism. The main difference in the two baptism is the personal commitment to Christ. (John 1:33, kjv, Acts 8:17, kjv) The Holy Spirit is the gift that comes with salvation. (Acts 2:38, kjv) The resurrection from water points to the Christian's resurrection. (Romans 6:1-6, kjv) But water apart from personal commitment to Christ means nothing in the life of anyone. Baptism has always been for believers. (Acts 2:38; 8:12-13, 36-38; Ephesians 4:5, kjv) We must accept Jesus as our Lord and Savior. Baptism is the cleansing by the Spirit of our God. (I Corinthians 6:11, kjv) Baptism of the Holy Spirit is also the seal of our salvation. (Ephesians 4:30, kjv) Along with baptism with the Holy Spirit come the ministry for which empowerment comes including witnessing spiritual gifts and knowledge in guidance. (John 14:26, 16:13, kjv)

On the subject of salvation, there is a need to examine the conditions under which it is offered. We all have sinned and come short of the glory of God. For the wages of sin is death, but the gift of God is eternal life through Jesus Christ, our Lord. (Romans 3:23, kjv) Salvation in its most basic sense will include deliverance from the penalty and power of sin. Because God is the source of our salvation any saving act is a spiritual event. In the case of personal salvation from sin God's act of forgiveness of the penitent can be found in scripture. Psalms 79:9; 85:4, 51:12, kjv The larger context of God's salvation can be read in Isaiah 25:9 that embraces the fact of an abundant life and the end of death, tears and disgrace (Isaiah 25:6, 8-9, kjv) that will be taken away from the earth. The prophets also spoke of a salvation that lay outside of the history of the nations. (Isaiah 51:6, kjv) In particular, the Psalms are especially interested in God's salvation of the "upright in heart" who rely on God for deliverance. (Psalms 36:10, 37:19-40, kjv) Salvation can be viewed from two perspectives, the shedding of blood for our sins and the believer's experience of salvation. The whole of Jesus's ministry was "to seek and save that which was lost". (Luke 19:10, kjv)

"God was in Christ reconciling the world to himself, not counting their trespasses against them". (II Corinthians 5:19, kjv) As a mediator Christ saving work deeply concerns those who wait for His return to bring salvation from the wrath of God's final judgment. (Romans 5:9-10, kjv) In the believer's life the initial work termed justification embraces God's final judgment. (Romans 2:13; 3:20-30, kjv) Sometimes referred to as God's finished work in the lives of all believers is His glorification. (Romans 8:17, kjv) Let us not forget that God's future work involves more than just individuals it extends to the renewal of heaven and earth. (Revelation 21:1, kjv) Scripture states that salvation is the free gift of God and is appropriated through faith. (Ephesians 2:8-9, Romans 3:28, kjv) Because of this no individual merit is involved that could fulfill God's law. (Romans 3:20, kjv) In keeping with the confidence of God's ability to keep us who have entrusted our lives to Christ should not be an excuse for believers to allow sin or moral deception to display itself in our lives. (Romans 6:12-13, kjv)

Chapter VI

THE RELATIONSHIP OF THIS JOINING TO REPENTANCE

In the reign of Josiah son of Amon who reigned thirty-one years in Jerusalem was one of the best Kings who reign after Solomon. He did that which was right in the sight of the Lord. (II Kings 22:2, kjv) He led a movement that became the greatest revival the people ever had after David and Solomon had passed. Some believe that the church today is under the blight of apostasy. That some portion of the word of God has been lost in the church. In the eighteenth year of King Josiah he sent Shapan the son of Azaliah to the house of the Lord to Hilkiah the high priest to sum up the offering from the people to repair the Temple. In the process of the repairs Hilkiah the high priest found the book of the law in the house of the Lord. (II Kings 22:8, kjv) Hilkiah had found the word of the Lord in the Temple where it had been lost. When this word was brought to King Josiah he was actually hearing the word of God for the first time. Scripture says that when he heard this he rent his clothes. (II Kings 22:11, kjv) The reading of the word of God brought repentance. It revealed their sins. Without the word of God they did not realize how far they had strayed from God's law. A revival and rejoicing relationship was becoming following a true repentance. Surely we can understand that our relationship, knowledge and purpose for joining the Word of God is important and begins with repentance.

In the book Ecclesiastes it states that "to him that is joined to all the living there is hope". (Ecclesiastes 9:4, kjv) we have something to look forward to in Christ who is the way, the truth and the life; "no man comes to the Father, but by me." (John 14:6: kjv) God's principal for joining has always been in hope and faith. So let us join ourselves to the Lord. (Jeremiah 50:55, kjv) For *"what God has joined together let not man put asunder." (Matthew 19:6, kjv)* Scripture states in the book of Acts that many signs and wonders were regularly done among the people of the Apostle. When they were all together in Solomon's Porch the people held them in high esteem and more then ever believers were added to the Lord, multitudes of both men and women. (Acts 5:12–14, kjv) But remember they were joined on one accord in the Lord. As we will learn in scripture, human wisdom divides the body. (I Corinthians 10-17, kjv) Question is, was Christ divided? Of course not. Therefore we should not allow the wisdom of words to separate us from the body of Christ. Let us not forget that we are saved by the power of God and His word. God says that He will destroy the wisdom of the wise, and will bring to nothing the understanding of the prudent. (I Corinthians 1:19, kjv) God has made foolish the wisdom of the world. (I Corinthians 1:20, kjv) It is important to remember that the whole body joined and held together by every joint with which it is equipped, when each part is working properly makes the body grow so that it builds itself up in love. (Ephesians 4:16, kjv)

The word "join" in the Greek is (Kallao) which means to join, unite closely" It is a reference to a person uniting or associating with other people. Paul in scripture challenges his readers to "cling to what is good" mainly Christ. (Romans 12:9, kjv) The binding nature of our joining is critical, finding its origin at creation. (Genesis 2:24, kjv) It must be kept from defilement. In God's activities the relationship is one of spiritual intimacy. The spiritual union to the believer is one within permanence and closeness to God. For he who unites himself with the Lord is one with him in the spirit. (I Corinthians 16:17, kjv) In other words, God is married to His Covenant people. They are not to defile the sanctity of such a relationship. *"Hear, O Israel; The Lord your God is one Lord" (Deuteronomy 6:4, kjv)* Because God is one, one set of laws applies to both Israelites and foreigners. (Numbers 15:16, kjv) The story of sin in human history is is a disruption of God's ordained unity. Starting with mistrust, accusations, stubbornness and hardness of heart. (Mark 10:5, kjv) However, the prophets hope of the future is that God will reunite all the people of the world under the sovereignty of the Lord. (Zechariah 14:9, kjv) A perfect example of unity was modeled by Jesus in His experience with the Father in scripture. (John 17:11, kjv) He prayed for unity to be realized in the life of the early church. What God has joined to together will overcome. The unity of the church reflects the unity of the Godhead. (I Corinthians 12:6, Kjv)

But he that is joined unto the Lord is one spirit.

— I Corinthians 6:17

Chapter VII

BE CAREFUL HOW WE PERCEIVE JOINING TOGETHER

We all know that Satan is a deceiver and this is one of his most powerful weapons against the children of God. As a deception he is always on the scene whenever we chose to obey God and His righteousness. Satan knows that how we perceive things has everything to do with our decision making and that some of us are weak in that area. This is why we need to stay in the Word of God and prayer in everything we do. As in scripture, Paul after receiving opposition from Satan was filled with the Holy Spirit, set his eyes on the sorcerer and said, *"O full of all deceit; and all mischief, thou child of the devil enemy of all righteousness, wilt thou not cease to pervert the right ways of the Lord?" (Acts 13:10, kjv) For there is a way that seems right to a man but the end thereof are the ways of death. (Proverbs 14:12, kjv)* We have to be careful how we relate and join ourselves to another. Ask ourselves, what is the reason I should want to join with this person or even associate with those whom we don't really know. Are there selfish benefits involved? Do you have much in common? There is a saying, "birds of a feather flock together." Bad choices are followed by bad connections. As a reminder scripture tells us *"to be ye unequally yoked with unbelievers." (II Corinthians 6:14, kjv)* Deception plays a big part in how we perceive a joining together.

THE BEGINNING OF OUR PERCEPTIONS

Our perception began with the fear of God on our lives. The teaching of this fear rooted from a child. (Proverb 22:6) Along with the requirements of the law and the importance of obedience, a foundation of living was established. How we perceive as a child begins to take form into life. As a child grows, his perception of life matures as he is guided by his beliefs and knowledge. Considering how carefully God cared for his people, when it came to choosing a mate. God had already prepared a reasonable source of male and female habitation that was an acceptable order for us to follow throughout future generations. That relationship, companionship or courtship should be done in respect to God's purpose for his people. First of all, the scriptures teach us that "can two walk together except they agree"? (Amos 3:3) So many young people have a perception that has not been nurtured or matured in the word of God and probably not their fault. They don't' even think that God even considers relationships since it is not the way they see it. Fact is, the whole word of God is about relationship and God is the one who instituted it. Considering a relationship out of a fleshly mind naturally is not of God and headed towards disaster. Relationships are not natural as some may think, but starts from our relationship with God. If we would ask ourselves is our relationship based on how we perceive it, or how we feel it? This is why we should consider the principles of a relationship provided by God. He is able to see far beyond your thoughts and knowledge into your future. He is able to see the whole picture that is not influenced by feelings, wishes and imaginations. Perceptions come in two realms, physical and spiritual. Regardless of what you think, why not have a relationship with God first and see the whole picture? God's purpose for a relationship is "Oneness". So many people have perceived that a relationship is about them and selfishly go after it for that purpose. Instead of using a spiritual perception they use a self perception. Sadly, enough they ended up with two different perceptions not on one accord. If your perceptions are not guided or nurtured by you, or those who know the word of God, you may be picking up some bad perception practices. This may be an awareness of who your friends really are. We have to be careful many times that our perceptions do not become judgments, because it is not what a person looks like, or how a situation seems to reveal itself. Be prayerful to be able to exercise your faith in God, as every situation is important because you have to act on it. Learn how to use your spiritual perceptibility.

PERCEPTIONS AND RELATIONSHIPS

Perceptions are realize in every area of our lives. Especially in our relationships with one another. One of the reason why we can't seem to get along with one another is because of the perception that we have of one another. We often have a tendency to judge one another where love is supposed to be present as well as respect for each other. Our view of our personal relationships seems to be taken over by our emotions, and looks towards another, rather than understanding the truth about each other. We are not taught, or guided by the purpose, and importance of our perceptions when it comes to choosing a mate or a friend. Instead of searching for truth or moral soundness, we allow our personal satisfaction to prevail over the circumstances for the moment. Relationships are not natural believe it or not, but have to be taught and guided just as well as our perceptions. Even though we do not naturally do this it is nevertheless necessary. Our lives can be wasted on a lot of bad decisions based on bad perceptions. If we just think about it, the whole world is having major problems with relationships, and making bad decisions to make it worth. Some would say we just don't love one another enough. But how can we love if we can't perceive what love is? (I Cor 12:1-7 KJV) if we would research scripture, we would find that some great lessons can be learned in the book of Genesis, in the Garden of Eden about relationships. Adam's first relationship was with God and when he sought a relationship with someone like himself, God brought to him Eve. When he saw Eve he said "Bone of my Bone, and flesh of my flesh" Which was to mean, she was like him to the point where the two of them would become one. (Gen

2:23 KJV) Adam's perception was clear and he knew that she was somebody whom he could relate to because she was given by God.

Adam's perception was clear before sin entered. But after the fall that perception became darkened. Today, God still provides the right perception for man, but it is man's responsibility to keep his vision clear from the deception of the Devil. It is so easy to perceive situations in the wrong way, usually depending on the condition of the heart. Most times we allow our emotions to determine our perceptions, true perceptions belong to the Holy Spirit. If we don't count on God to guide our perceptions and keep our vision clear, we will fail in our predictions of our relationships. We must have a relationship with God first in order to have a right relationship with another. God is the relationship maker, keeper, and protector. He is the one who created relationship. The whole Bible is about relationships. If we take the chance on entering a relationship without perceiving the whole picture based on God's word, we will fail. We are not born with good perceptions, therefore we must depend on God. I have introduced these principles in my recent book "What we don't understand about relationships."

In any relationship, our perceptions are expected to be highly reliable especially in our decision making. It is very discouraging and painful to find out that you were wrong in your perception about a relationship that meant a lot to you personally. But even though it happens, often people overlook the error not really understanding why that was possible when they were so easily persuaded that they could perceive that happening. Sometimes we blame ourselves; sometimes we blame the other person. But the real disappointment is when we wish we could have prevented the problem. We never consider that perceptions or communication had anything to do with the problem. There is no perfect way to perceive a situation since we are not in control of understanding our environment or other perceptions.

In the book of Matthew Jesus asked Peter "who do men say that I, the Son of man am?" And Peter said thou art the Christ, the Son of the living God. Jesus answered and said unto him, "Blessed art thou Simon Bar-jo-na; for flesh and blood hath not revealed it unto thee, but my Father, who is in heaven." In other words, Peter did not perceive that physically but God, the Father gave him that perception spiritually. An example of the kind of relationship Jesus wants us to have with the father that we can trust Him with the truth. If we would just trust God in the spirit he will guide our perceptions into all truth. (John 16:13)

As I mentioned earlier, the biggest problem with the world is relationship, we can't get along with each other. We are still remaining in darkness and trying to make light out of it. We are trying to perceive in the flesh that which can only be seen in the spirit and trusting in it. God wants us to be happy, but happiness is not in the things we can perceive, but in the things that we can't see or understand. (LK 12:15b) We exist for God's purposes and not ours. It is because of God that we live and breathe, and have our being. (Gen 2:7, Acts 17:28) Therefore, we should seek ye first the Kingdom of God and his Righteousness. (Matt 6:33) This should be our first relationship for righteousness. Your perception will become clear along with your understanding of your purpose. You will no longer perceive things selfishly, but in the Spirit of God and His word.

CHAPTER VIII

SEALED WITH THE HOLY SPIRIT OF PROMISE

The Holy Spirit of Promise confirms us as acceptable to God the righteous acts, ordinances and covenants of men. The Holy Spirit of Promise witness to the Father that the saving ordinances have been and will be performed. (Acts 2:33, kjv) God's announcement of His plan of salvation and blessing to His people was one of the unifying themes that integrated the message along with the deeds in the Old and New Testament. The promise embraced both the declaration and the deed. It covered not only one race but all the nations of the earth. It included the gifts and the deeds that God bestowed on a few to benefit many. God's promise can be defined as the divine declaration or assurance to Eve, Shem, Abram, Isaac and Jacob and of course the whole nation of Israel. Stating that He would be their God, they would be His people and He would dwell with them. God's promises were eternal. The promises of the Holy Spirit appears after our Lord's resurrection (Luke 24:49; Acts 2:33, 38-39, kjv) The Holy of Promise simply means that the Holy Spirit will place the stamp of approval upon every ordinance, baptism, confirmation, ordination and marriage. That the blessings will be received through faithfulness. And carry with it security, authenticity, ownership and authority. *"In whom ye also trusted, after ye heard the word of truth, the gospel of your salvation; in whom also after ye believed, ye were sealed with the Holy Spirit of Promise" (Ephesians 1:13, kjv) "who is the earnest of our inheritance until the redemption of the purchased possession, unto the praise of His glory." (Ephesians 1:14, kjv)*

Spiritual gifts given to Christians of God equips them to serve God and the Christian community. In the Old Testament these gifts were given to selected leaders rather than for all of God's people. To serve Israel these gits were used for example:

bezalee}, who was given the gift of craftsmanship (Exodus 31:2-3, kjv) Othaniel, who was equipped to be a judge; (Judges 10, kjv) Gideon, was given military skills; (Judges 6:34, kjv) Samson, who was given great physical strength; (Judges 14:6, 19, kjv) Saul, had been given political knowledge; (1 Samuel 10:6, kjv) then there was Micah, who received prophetic gifts; (Micah 3:8, kjv) The Christian view of spiritual gifts or promises begins with Jesus who was the unique bearer of the Spirit. (Mark 1:10, kjv) Jesus promised His disciples that they would also receive the Spirit one day and be guided by that Spirit. (Mark 13:11, kjv) These promises were filled on the day of Pentecost. (Acts 2:1-47, kjv) The Holy Spirit of *Promise is "earnest of our inheritance until the redemption of the purchased possession, until the praise of His glory." (Ephesians 1:14, kjv) All Christians are* given gifts. (I Corinthians 12:4-7, kjv) Love is the ultimate spiritual gift and most important.

In the New Testament concerning the promise to the inviolable and precious, *it states "Where in God, willing more abundant to show unto the heirs of promise the immutability of His counsel, confirmed it by an oath." That by two immutable* things, in which it was impossible for God to lie, we might have a strong consolation who have fled for a refuge today hold upon the hope set before us,"

(Hebrew 6:17-18, kjv) "*Also* by which *are given unto* as *exceedingly great and precious promises, that by these ye might be partakers of the divine nature, having escaped the corruption that is in the world through lust." (II Peter 1:4, kjv) in* hope of eternal life, which God who cannot lie, promised before the world began. (Titus 1:2, kjv) And for those who have repented and returning to the *Lord, God says* "*Come out from among them, and be ye separated, saith the Lord and touch not the unclean thing; and I will receive you, and will be a Father unto you, and ye shall be my sons and daughters, saith the Lord Almighty*" *(II Corinthians 6:17-18, kjv)* Anointed believers will receive the Holy Spirit of Promise according to our Lord and Savior Jesus Christ. "*in* whom ye *also trusted, after ye hear the word of truth, the gospel of your salvation; in whom also after ye believed, ye were sealed with the Holy Spirit of Promise.* (Ephesians 1:13-14)

Come, and let us join ourselves to the Lord in a perpetual covenant that shall not be forgotten.

— Jeremiah 50:5

Chapter IX

LET US JOIN OURSELVES TO THE LORD

In the prophecy against Babylon, the Lord spoke against Babylon and the land of the Chaldaens through Jeremiah the prophet saying to declare among the nations and publish a standard that her idols and images are confounded and broken in pieces. That her land will become desolate. And in those saith the Lord, the children of Israel and Judah shall come together seeking their God. They shall ask the way of Zion saying *"Come and let us join ourselves to the Lord in a perpetual Covenant that shall not be forgotten." (Jeremiah 50:1-5. kjv)* Even though this was a actual prophecy, it was truth. Today as then God's people are still lost sheep that have gone astray. (Isaiah 53:6, kjv) *"We have turned everyone to his own way, and the Lord hath laid on him the iniquity of us all." (Isaiah 53:6, kjv)* The cause for this lost was charged to their shepherds who turned them away on the mountains going from there to hills; they had forgotten their resting place which was in the Lord. (Jeremiah 50:6, kjv) The consequence for turning their backs on the Lord in sin resulted in, *"Thus saith the Lord God: Feed the flock of the slaughter whose possessor slay them, and hold themselves not guilty."* In other words, the Lord would aid their enemy to the point to where they themselves would not count themselves guilty for what they had done. (Zechariah 11:4-5, kjv) Even their own shepherds pitied them not. Even the Lord says *"I will no more pity the inhabitants of the land but, lo, I will deliver the men, every one, into his neighbor's hand, and into the hand of his king; and they shall smite the land, and out of their hand I will not deliver them."* *(Zechariah 11:5-6, kjv)* The Romans would credit God for the gain they received in their abuse of Israel while God was sponsoring their consequences. While they rejected the Messiah, their rightful King, God delivered them into the hands of Caesar. The judgment of God will be completed embracing the entire land with no way out. The message is loud and clear according to Jeremiah, *"let us join ourselves to the Lord in a perpetual Covenant that shall not be forgotten".* *(Jeremiah 50:5, kjv)* While the spotlight is on obedience and considering the fact that God has given us His laws, we are reminded that as Paul says *"by the name of our Lord Jesus Christ, that ye all speak the same thing, and that there be no divisions among you, but that ye be perfectly joined together in the same mind and in the same judgment. (I Corinthians 1:10, kjv)* This is no less the responsibility of our shepherds to guide us in the way of the Lord. *"From whom the whole body fitly joined together and compacted by that which every joint supplieth, according to the effectual working in the measure of every part, maketh increase of the body unto the edifying of itself in love." (Ephesians 4:16, kjv)* We have been invited to participate in one of the most holy unified and eternal rest in the body of our Lord and Savior Jesus Christ. Who says, *"Come unto me, all ye that labor and are heavy laden, and I will give you rest." (Matthew 11:28, kjv)* God works in mysterious ways and so does His love. As *"for him that is joined to all living there is hope". (Ecclesiastes 9:4, kjv)* But let us not forget that *"though hand join in hand the wicked shall not be unpunished; but the seed of the righteous shall be delivered. (Proverbs 11:21, Kjv)* God gave us a Covenant to join with Him in obedience and love. He did not give us a compromise. It was for our benefit as He had reminded us in the pass. That once we had come into the lands filled with milk and honey don't forget about the Lord. (Deuteronomy 6:10-12, kjv) He is still the object of our faith that we depend upon which is Jesus Christ our Lord and Savior. And we believe that *"there is no other name under heaven given among men, whereby we must be saved."* *(Act 4:12, kjv)*

Chapter X

HE THAT IS JOINED TO
THE LORD IS ONE SPIRIT

The Bible declares that the Lord our God is one. *"Hear, O Israel: the Lord our God is one Lord". (Deuteronomy 6:4, kjv)* He is equal in every divine perfection as in the trinity that is the Father, Son and the Holy Spirit. In the unity of the Godhead He executes distinct but harmonious works in the area of redemption. (Matthew 1:21, kjv) (Ephesians 2:8, 9, kjv; Titus 3:5, kjv) We praise God for the glory of His grace though which he made us accepted in the

Beloved in whom we have redemption through His blood, the forgiveness of sins according to the riches of His grace. (Ephesians 1:6, 7, kjv) In the book of John in the scriptures it states that Jesus prayed to the Father on behalf of His disciples according to the faith that they say they have in the word of God and also those who believe saying, *"Neither pray for these alone, but for them also who shall believe on me through their work," that they all may be one as thou, Father art in me, and I in thee; that they also may be one in us; that the world may believe that thou hast sent me. And the glory which thou gavest me. I have given them, that they may be one, even as we are one; (John 17:20-22. kjv)*

Clearly oneness with God is the greatest opportunity we are privileged to have spiritually. But in the absence of God's grace we have nothing and are lost. Imagine the Creator of the universe, the omnipotent, omniscience and omnipresent God is in the business of trying to love you and be with you forever. *"Even before the foundation of the world He hath chosen us in him before the foundation of the world, that we should be holy and without blame before him in love".* *(Ephesians 1:5, kjv)* For the time is coming when "the Lord himself shall descend from heaven with a shout, with the voice of the archangel, and with the trump of God; and the dead in Christ shall rise first; then who are alive and remain shall be caught up with them in the clouds, to meet the Lord in the air; and so shall we ever be with the Lord." (I Thessalonians 4:16–17, kjv) Then shall we ever be one with the Lord.

But we don't have to wait to until His return to be one with the Lord. We should join ourselves to the Lord right now while the blood runs warm in our veins. *"For God hath not appointed us to wrath but to salvation by our Lord Jesus Christ. (I Thessalonians 5:9, kjv)* Being of one spirit may be confusion in some passages where "soul" and "spirit" are used interchangeably when referring to man. There is a distinction that is declared to be divisible. (Hebrew 4:12, kjv) When referring to the burial and resurrection of the body that is buried and naturally (GK *soma psuchikon-soul) that is raised a spirit body (GK soma pneumatikon) (I Corinthians 15:44, kjv)* The difference in the two terms is that the spirit is that which "knows" (I Corinthians 2:11, kjv) and has God consciousness and communication with God. (Job 32:8, Proverbs 20:27, kjv) When we join ourselves to the Lord we join as one spirit. Even so after sharing the death burial and resurrection *of Jesus Christ.*

For To Him That Is Joined To All
The Living There Is Hope

— Ecclesiastes 9:4

Chapter XI

PRONOUNCEMENT OF JUDGMENT

As the result of not listening and refusal to do, despising and abhoring God's statues and judgments brought judgment upon the people and the land according to the book of Leviticus. The prophets in their messages had called their attention to the fact that they had broken the covenant which God had made with them. In other words they were being disobedient and brought punishment upon themselves (Leviticus 26:16–39, kjv) The future of

God's people rests upon the solid history of the past when God delivered them from Egypt. And "He who hath done a good work in you will perform it until the day of Jesus Christ." (Philippians 1:6. kjv) A chastising relationship will always be among God's people.

In the preparation of Moses death in referring to the time he smote the rock twice after God had told him to speak to it. God said clearly that this was rebellion against His commandment. Because Moses did this he was only allowed to view the promised land and not enter except after his death on the mount of transfiguration with the Lord Jesus. (Mathew 17:3, kjv) The book of Numbers 27:12-14 is another example of how God deals with our obedience on an individual level as well as leadership. God is no respecter of persons. This also means that disobedience can keep us from entering our spiritual possessions and disbelief will always lead to disobedience. At the end of king Solomon's reign God began to stir up trouble on him through the dividing of the kingdom because of taking on other wives and worship of other gods. There became no peace only warfare. (I Kings 11:11-14, kjv) Keep in mind that God had a plan for the future kingdom of David and his kingdom which included the tribe of Judah and the tribe of Benjamin. (I Kings 11:9-13, kjv) The chastising relationship of God is consistent throughout scripture as we look at Job. God gives reference to Job saying to him that in the days past when he was in prosperity and plenty and good health how he was a tower of strength to everyone. He could advise everyone what to do and was wise. He knew how to help those in trouble but now he has change. Its like he was never real at all. The advice he gave to others he could not follow.

Its interesting how we can tell other people what to do about their problems but when it comes to you, you fold up. If your advice can help others it ought to help you. God does not give advice He gives wisdom. Scripture states "happy is the man that God correcteth therefore despise not thou the chastening of the Almighty." (Job 5:17, kjv) Chastening is not always the reason that God's people suffer. Sometimes people may use this verse and understanding to persuade others the reason they suffer as Eliphaz made an excuse for a suffering. In other words you have done something wrong and God is correcting you. You are making a judgment call that could turn your heart away from God's purpose. Application of the reason for suffering belongs to God. He is in control of purpose and reason not man. As the Psalmist says, "Blessed is the man whom thou Chasteneth, O

Lord, and teacheth him out of thy law". (Psalms 94:12, kjv) After all, "He who teacheth man knowledge, shall not he know?" (Psalms 94:10, kjv) There is only two places for your sins. They are on you or they are on Christ. Think about the future judgment.

Whether you understand it or not if you are God's child He is going to chasten you as you go through life. Even though He may not touch the devil's children but He will correct His own. Thats how we know He loves us as His children and belong to Him. Chastening is not punishing as some think. Punishing is for criminals chastening is for children. Our children should be corrected first and then disciplined. This Is what God requires of His children.

Remember, chastening is not punishing. We punish a criminal, we correct a child. Our children are to be corrected and disciplined. This is what God requires of His children. "A whip for the horse, a bridle for the ass, and a rod for the fool's back. (Proverbs 26:3, kjv) A horse and ass can be trained and will respond but a fool will only respond to real discipline. Many times parents depend upon the beating to do the correcting rather than the teaching and correcting. Many times the children don't know why they are being beaten because they were not taught or corrected before hand. Did you teach them not to do what they are being beaten for? Or did you summarize every bad behavior into one correct response?

Wisdom is suppose the be the guide along with examples for correction. This is why children are more concerned about the beating than the correction even with understanding. "Foolishness is bound in the heart of a child, but the rod of correction shall drive it far from him".

(Proverbs 22:15, kjv) Proper discipline will help the child overcome his foolishness. For God said that He would not have us ignorant. "Correct thy son, and he shall give thee rest; yea, he shall give delight unto thy soul." (Proverbs 29:17, kjv) This is the importance of discipline.

During the time of Jacob's trouble in the book of Jeremiah the Lord said, "For I am with thee, saith the Lord, to save thee; though I make a full end of all nations to which I have scattered thee, yet will I not make a full end of thee, but I will correct thee in measure, and will not have thee altogether unpunished. (Jeremiah 30:11, kjv) The Lord has promised to deal with Israel as his sons when it comes to discipline in a just and loving way. We should take this personally when it comes to certain things that happens to us in life. When we set down for a providence asking ourselves what is the purpose of this happening to us. We should consider that whether the situation is good or bad to us it is still the providence of God. We are always preserved whether it is just or unjust it is ordered by God. It is written "I form light and create darkness, I make peace and create evil. I the Lord do all these thing". (Isaiah 45:7, kjv) We have put ourselves many times on the mount of assurance only to find that we have only realized that we have put ourselves in the valley of humiliation because we have not understood God's providence and that He is in control. It would appear that everything is against us. But no, "now, you are despising the chastening of the Lord, when you say this is of no use. No child thinks the rod is of any value. Chastening is not considered as part of a relationship when it comes to discipline, so you say. In considering, how many men have thought that it was dishonorable to be persecuted for righteousness sake? For the Bible says "they that shall live righteous shall suffer persecution" (II Timothy 3:12, kjv) nevertheless, the question is, do we have a choice of how, where and when that persecution is to come. We leave out the will of God and His providence of our lives because it is against our own displeasure.

We don't expect to enter tribulation except it be a judgment call or earnest of it. Actually it is the glory of a man to be chastened for God's sake. Some men never earnestly seek to amend by the chastening of the Lord. They have been corrected by God but that correction has been in vain. These are Christian men who have been shown the sin and never afterwards corrected it. This is despising the chastening of the Lord. If you repeat the sin after chastened you are despising the chastening of the Father. Remember it is only a sanctified affliction that benefit the Christian. And it is not every trial that purifies only a trial that God himself sanctifies by His grace. We should take the time to look at the causes of our afflictions. We should also observe those around us that God chastened it could be a warning for you. The most chastened of God are usually the most to benefit from. Do not be ashamed to talk with the chastened ones and don't put them off because of their poverty.

"Nor faint when thou art rebuked of Him." (Hebrews 12:5, kjv) This statement relates to us in several ways that we may faint under the afflicting hand of God. After serving the Lord in many different ways suddenly we stop and make excuses because we cannot enjoy all the comforts we want we will not do anything. And by allowing ourselves to be influenced by Satan and conscience we then feel like we have lost our Christianity and begin to doubt we are a child of God. "My son, faint not when thou art corrected of Him." God does not like gloomy children, and there are many of his children fainting out of moods. All because God does not do them pleasure, they do nothing at all. They feel that they must be in front at all times. Instead of moving forward and not fainting we should accept the lasher. I should make an effort to get away from the rod by accepting the correction to the right pass. Father please forgive me of my transgressions and doubts and help me to realize who I am in the faith. Strengthen me of my thoughts and restore my spirit of faith according to your will. We have been fainting and telling ourselves we are not a child of God because we should be in poverty and distress. Believe it or not the trials are proof that we have been adopted by the Father and are on our way to the Kingdom of heaven. "If we are not partakers of chastisement then we are bastards, and not sons." (Hebrews 12:7, kjv)

Many children faint because they think they will not get out of their troubles. They forgot that God never told them to solve their own problems. We have got to stop thinking that life is on our time clock. It is that thinking that has led us away from God's promises. Have we considered that God always gives us what we need to overcome the afflictions? In all actuality is there such a son that has not been chastened by the Father? No, not one; there is not one in heaven whose back was unscared by the chastening rod. "Remember the chastisement of our peace is upon him he suffered; he bore the cross; he endured the curse more than any of us; even more chastisement than any of us. So, "My son, despise not the chastening of the Lord, neither faint when thou art rebuked of him". (Hebrews 12:5. kjv)

In closing my heart goes out to those who are afflicted but have not religion to comfort them to make a choice of faith. Christians know that they are children of God and that these afflictions are for their own good. Where do you get comfort from? I can see when the glass is full hearts are glad and joyous but what do you do when the glass is empty and there is pain. Who do you call? Trust Jesus

"And ye have forgotten the exhortation which speaketh unto you as unto sons, My son, despise not thou the chastening of the Lord, nor faint when thou are rebuked of him;

— Hebrews 12:5, kjv

Chapter XII

THE CHASTENING
OF THE LORD

Since God has already punished the children of God completely in the person of our Lord and Savior Jesus Christ. Children of God cannot possibly be punished again for their sins. Jesus as their substitute has endured the required penalty for all their guilt. It never has to be paid again what Christ has paid in full. Therefore a child of God cannot be punished again in the legal sense and be brought before God as his judge and being charged with guilt, because of what Christ has done. But even though the sin cannot be punished we can be chastised, but stand in a new relationship with God the Father as a son may be chastened on account of sin. Scripture states that folly is bound up in the heart of all God's children but the rod of correction shall drive it far from him. (Proverbs 22:15, kjv) If we would observe the distinction between punishment and chastisement, the one suffering can be as great as the other. There is no more punishment for guilt in this life of the sinner than the Christian that is chastised by his parents. There is no difference in the nature of the punishment but in the mind of the punisher and the relationship of the person who is punished. God's justice must be avenged and His law honored. But He does not punish the believer on his own account but on the Christian's account. God has a good design and guiding towards the person who receives the chastisement. God always receives the glory in chastisement. Punishment is laid on man because of God's anger and is always applied in love. Before the rod is laid to the believer's back it is baptized in deep affection with the wisdom of God. (Proverbs 10:13, kjv)

We should never say "God must be punishing me for my sin" The truth is God cannot do that. He has done it once and for all. Scripture states that the chastisement of our peace was upon Him and with His stripes we are healed. (Isaiah 53:5, kjv) "He that spareth the rod hateth his son". (Proverbs 13:24, kjv) He is chastising thee, not punishing thee; this is a correcting measure not a smiting in wrath. In considering the person of Christ He seeth no sin in Jacob nor iniquity in

Israel because he loves his sons. This is why He chastises them.

Two dangers should a child of God under the chastening of the Lord be aware of and careful. "My son despise not thou the chastening of the Lord and "Neither faint when thou art rebuked of him". (Hebrew 12:5, kjv) There always seems to be two challenges on the opposite side of one another when it comes to the way of righteousness and leads to a difficult pass between two great places of error. The Christian life continues to travel through this valley with the help of God's presence. One of the first responses as Christians being chastened by the hand of God is we despise or even faint when he is rebuked. He begins by murmuring at it not being used to being resisted or told he is wrong and not able to bear the collar put upon his shoulders. But turns to the Father and questions his action

towards him like, "Why am I punished
and afflicted?" What have I done to
deserve this?" Comparing our afflictions
and punishments with other Christians
to justify our merit. Accusing God the
Father of not dealing with us with a just
cause, as if God owes us anything more
than love. We have a tendency to put
our own condition in the worst place,
and describe ourselves as being the most
afflicted of all God's people. Right now
there murmurers in the midst of Israel
who are people of God until the rod
falls, cry out against it instead of kissing
the Son lest he be angry, turn against
the affliction dispensation of God. For
scripture states that "no chastening for the
present seemeth to be joyous but grievous,
nevertheless, afterwards it yieldeth the
peaceable fruit of righteousness unto them
who are exercised by it." (Hebrew 12:11,
kjv) "My son despise not the chastening

of the Lord, neither be weary of his correction; For whom the Lord loveth he correcteth, even as a father the son in whom he delighteth. (Proverbs 3:11-12, kjv)

Hey, murmurer, who do you think you are? Why would you murmur against the dispensation of thy heavenly Father? Do you think he is treating you any worst than you deserve? Look at the way you have acted most of your life and the Father has pardoned you and you still rebel. What do you think you deserve? You certainly don't have the right to complain since the wages of sin is death and you are still exercising opportunity to serve him. Do you not remember that the Roman emperors of old would by custom strike a slave in the head before setting a slave at liberty and say, go, you are free?

By the same token the Father gives token of thy liberty, and you complain because it was a little hard? Do you really think your strokes compares to the crimes and guilt you carried? That proud spirit of yours proves that your heart is not thoroughly sanctified; and though it may be right with God, your words do not sound like it and your actions do not profess the holiness of thy nature. God will give us something to cry about if we don't be patient at his discipline. So be not angry with the Lord because he is not angry with you. He loves you.

*"And ye have forgotten the exhortation
which speaketh unto you as unto
sons, My son, despise not thou the
chastening of the Lord, nor faint
when thou are rebuked of him;*

— Hebrews 12:5, kjv

Chapter XIII

THE PROVIDENCE OF GOD

This is God's faithful and effective care and guidance of everything which He has made and chosen until the end of time as He has chosen. In the Heidelberg Catechism (1563) a question was asked: What is your only comfort in life and death? And the answer was that in body and soul life and death are not my own but belong to my faithful Savior Jesus Christ who has preserved me so that without the will of my heavenly Father, not a hair can fall from my head and that all things must work together for salvation. This statement gets to the heart of the biblical doctrine of providence. By this we understand we can distinguish the meaning of providence from several distortions during the history of the church. In the New Testament, the Greek word for providence *(pronia)* occurs only once, and that with reference to human rather than divine foresight. (Acts 24:2, kjv) The verbal form *(proneo)* meaning "to know in advance" is found twice in the New Testament and eleven times In the Greek Old Testament according to bible dictionaries. But of course the theme of God's provident care for the created order is present in all levels of the biblical material. The Psalms are filled with allusion to God's directions and cause of creation. The heavens declares the glory of God, and the firmament showeth His handiwork. (Psalms 19:1, kjv) He appointed the moon for seasons the sun knoweth its going down. (Psalms 104:19, kjv) Everything that has breath is exhorted praise the Lord "for His mighty acts" (150; 2, 6, kjv) Providence is related to creation on one hand and the history of salvation on the other. This is known as the second aspect of "special" providence to Theologians. In Nehemiah 9:6–38, God brings together His general and special providence in the same passage. After the destruction of Jerusalem in 587 B. C. and the long period of exile, confidence in God's providence sustained the children of Israel through all of their doubts and disappointments. Despite the fact that there still exits the influence of "Deism" the idea that God created the world but then withdrew from it from day to day governance, leaving it to run by itself as a machine. It is believed by those in "Deism" that it safeguards the transcendence of God at the expense of His imminence. There was also the belief of pantheism, that was the opposite error of deism, it virtually identifies God with His creation. God is a kind of world soul or impersonal force which permeates all the universe. And last but not least there was the influence of "Dualism" a view that two opposing forces in the universe are locked in a struggle with each other for its control. The ancient religions Zoroaster and Mani posited two co-eternal principles, darkness and light. A belief that God is limited by the evolving universe and caught in a struggle with forces over control. There two passages in the New Testament direct Christians to focus on God's providential care as a remedy for overanxious concern. In the sermon on the mount, Jesus told His hearers not to worry about tomorrow and that the heavenly Father cared much more for them than the birds of the air or the lillie of the field, Matthew 6:25-34, kjv) What this provides is the assurance of God's presence in the midst of what ever we face God will care for us as He does for everything else. Because we know that all things work for the good of those who love him and are called according to His purpose. (Romans 8:28, kjv) This does not mean that everything that happens to us is good but that nothing will happen to us unless God permits it according to His loving purpose. We must remember that the sufferings of the present time are not worst comparing with the glory that is to be revealed to us. (Romans 8:18-25, kjv)

The doctrine of providence encompasses many other themes in the Bible as well. God works in mysterious ways especially in His will. He has a sovereign will, a permissive will and a perfect will. Remember, nothing in all creation will be able to separate us from the love of God in Christ Jesus our Lord "(Romans 8:39, kjv) The fact that God created all things by His power and for His glory may be considered an established fact. What is commonly called Providence, the Providence of God, is suggested by creation, and may be inferred from it. In God's economy creation and preservation are inseparable. (Nehemiah 9:6, kjv) In the book of Job 7:20 God is recognized as the "Preserver of man" and in Psalms 36:6, kjv it reads "O Lord, thou preserveth man and beast." The eyes of all wait upon thee and thou givest them their meat in due season. The providential preservation is not only confined to this world but to all worlds. When it comes to the understanding of time and place of death the best understanding we can have is it has been so ordered by God. Regardless of our wills our lives have been so ordered, "It is appointed onto men once to die." (Hebrews 9:27, kjv) The appointment is inevitable and universal. Especially all who are "born of women."

The doctrine of providence is full of consolation to the saints. They are assured that the world as well as the universe is not the result of unreasoning dominion of fate or blind chances as some philosophers believe. Fate and chances are impersonal things, there is no life or intelligence in them. We have a personal God on the throne of the universe, an infinite intelligent Spirit worthy of all possible honor confidence and love. "For the eyes of the Lord run to and fro throughout the whole earth, to shew himself strong in the behalf of them whose heart is perfect toward Him. (II Chronicle 16:9, kjv) Love and wisdom control the arm and its power is exerted in the interest of His saints; "For the Lord God is a sun and shield: the

Lord will give grace and glory; no good thing will He withhold from them that walk uprightly." Psalms 84:11, kjv) It is a precious truth that sits upon a throne, wielding a universal sceptre making all things to work together for the good of those who love Him. All Christian will be comforted. There will be a solution of the mysteries of providence. "Because now I know in part," the present state of being is imperfect and unfinished and therefore needs be supplemented by the future and final state. When this occurs "then shall I know even as also I am known." (I Corinthians 13:12, kjv) The doctrine of scripture states that "He holdeth back the face of His throne, and spreadeth His cloud upon it." Thy way is in the sea, and thy path is in the great waters, and thy footsteps are not known." (Psalms 77:19, kjv) "clouds and darkness are around about Him." (Psalms 97:2, kjv) "What I do thou knowest not now, but thou shall know thereafter." (John 13:7, kjv)

The Psalmist was so perplexed by the prosperity of the wicked that in a moment of loss of courage and hope he said "verily. I have cleaned my heart in vain." (Psalms 73:13, kjv) Also in Jeremiah 12:1, kjv, the perplexity of Jeremiah was in substance the same, "Righteous art thou, O Lord, when I plead with thee yet let me talk with thee of thy judgment: Wherefore do the wicked prosper? Wherefore are all they happy that deal very treacherously? (Jeremiah 12:1, kjv)

Even Jacob in his lifetime saw the mistake he had made that the things were not for him that he thought was against him. He saw that the selling of his brother Joseph into slavery would be overruled for the preservation of the chosen race. We can realize from this that the solution of most dark providence is transferred and deferred to the future state. It is a triumphant and vindication of the ways of God. Then we will see that our "light afflictions," which only last for a moment, worketh for us a far more exceeding and eternal weight of glory." (II Corinthians 4:17, kjv) Scripture teaches us that as Christians we should never give up. For it has been promised that "he who has raised up the Lord Jesus shall raise us also by Jesus, and shall present us with you. "For all things are your sakes, that the abundant grace might through the thanksgiving of many redound to the glory of God." For which cause we faint not, but though our outward man perish, yet the inward man is renewed day by day. (II Corinthians 4:14-16, kjv) So let us not be weary in well doing; for in due season we shall reap, if we faint not. (Galatians 6:9, kjv)

Chapter XIV

TRIALS AND TRIBULATIONS

The phrase trials and tribulations carries the meaning, problems, difficulties, and tests. Who desires these? Nobody. It is commonly used in religious settings as well as older generations to raise our attention to a level of struggle unwanted. While there are new challenge in the post modern age we now live in, the essence of suffering remains the same, a separation from God. It has been said that the psychological suffering of Christians as well as the sin today will parallel the physical trials of the early Christian martyrs. Sometimes hard times is the only way we will get the message. (Galatians 6:7, kjv) The temptation of pride had been around since Adam and Eve. When it comes to the understanding of chastisement we must recall our relationship if any with Christ and know that we are never alone and that that relationship requires a choice at all times to being obedient to the Father. God is in control and knows all and sees all. And we all are subject to His purpose for our lives. Therefore, there is a reason why we suffer usually because of circumstances, bad choices or when things don't go our way. While we claim pride as being our priority that does not give us control or authority over our lives. God will be glorified.

In the book of John 16:33, kjv it states "In the world ye shall have tribulations:

but be of good cheer; I have overcome the world." Jesus has overcome the world of trials and tribulations for us. Even though we continue to struggle and are tested daily we are always in the presence of God. As a child of God we can pray and receive comfort and answers to our problems. We must learn to trust in the one who has all power and is in control of everything and everything is in His purpose. Nobody wants to be tested all the time for fear of failure but our testing believe it or not is to strengthen our faith and trust in God. It helps us to build a stronger relationship with our Lord and Savior Jesus Christ.

For as much as we may not understand why we suffer, remember we are sharing the death, burial and resurrection of Jesus Christ. God is not punishing us for our sins but correcting us for our wrong decisions and choices. It is indeed a challenge for us to perceive trials and tribulations as being productive, nevertheless they are ordered by God should you be a child of God. If we would live a life of prayer and try to understand God's purpose for our lives we would have a better relationship with Him. God loves us and what we are experiencing are examples of His love that cares for our character. Even those who don't know God in the pardon of their sins can learn that their lives are not about them but about the power of God onto salvation. We live in a sin cursed world filled with trials and tribulations and because we don't have Jesus the light of the world we are influenced to challenge darkness on our own. Not realizing that we are not fighting with flesh and blood but with principalities and rulers of darkness in high places. (Ephesians 6:12) This is spiritual warfare and your perceptions have been darkened from seeing the truth. God has never told us to fight this war or solve our problems on our own but to bring all of our cares to Him as children to the Father. (I Peter 5:7, kjv) Nothing can happen to us in our lives unless God allows it. No pain, no suffering, no sickness, or even death unless God allows it. He is in control of everything. The word of God is more powerful than any thought or act. We have been chosen even before the foundation of the world. (Ephesians 1:4, kjv) God knows what we were going to face in our lives thats why He says He would never leave us. (Matthew 28:20, kjv) So rather than being concerned about our trials and tribulations lets concern ourselves with our obedience to God's word as children of God. (Matthew 11:29, kjv) The world is a challenge because it is not our home. It is a place of journey and preparation. Everybody has to make choices and chooses a path. There will certainly be temptations and deceptions because the adversary who is Satan seeks to destroy you every chance he gets. Imagine how different troubling situations have on your character in the way that you respond. Imagine how all your life you have responded to different situations in different ways depending on the way you felt about that situation at that time.

Ask yourself what kind of character would you have become or how would you handle your problems if never satisfied? So people say we learn by experience but what did you learn? And what was the benefit? Was this learning righteousness or personal satisfaction? Whatever you understood it will not prepare you for the next trial or tribulation. We need the word of God in our lives that teaches us love and dependence upon Him. That lets us know He can solve all of our problems and that we need to prepare for it by letting Him control our lives and our situations.

"Blessed is the man who walketh not in the counsel of the ungodly, nor standeth in the way of sinners, nor sitteth in the seat of the scornful. But his delight is in the law of the Lord and in his law doth he meditate day and night". (Psalms 1:12)

God never asked us to understanding everything. Thats impossible but we can except the one who does know everything and understands all things. God says "counsel is mine, and, sound wisdom." I am understanding; I have strength. (Proverbs 8:14, kjv)

We need to change our perception and realize that every situation in this world and in our lives is a trial and has a purpose with God. God created it that way. Struggling to have your way will fail every time. God did not give you this world. He gave you life. He gave you a covenant not a compromise. He gave you dominion over the earth and an opportunity to praise Him. He paid for our sins and promised to love you and never leave you alone. We must realize that we can't earn anything from God and that all of our goodness is as filthy rags. (Isaiah 64:6, kjv) If we stop and think about it, most of our trials and tribulations were brought upon ourselves because of bad choices and lack of knowledge. Nevertheless, the Lord always demonstrates His mercy through prayers. We all have goals in life and we expect to reach those goals if we play the rules and wisdom of man as if he is in control. But God says that "In all your ways acknowledge Him and He shall direct your path." (Proverbs 3:6, kjv) This is a guarantee not a wish. We must understand that just because we receive blessings doesn't mean that we know how to manage them. We should realize that these things come from God. (Romans 8:28, kjv) Remember trials and tribulations will always be a part of our lives whether we are Christians or not. They serve God's purpose and is another productive way of demonstrating His love for His children. In the book of James in scripture it states, "my brethren, count it all joy when you fall into various trials, knowing this, that the testing of your faith worketh patient. "but let patience have her perfect work, that ye may be perfect and entire, lacking nothing." (James 1:4, kjv) If we would ask ourselves where about does the strength of our faith develop? We would understand the purpose of trials and tribulations. The purpose of trials and tribulations lies in the understanding of who He is and what our relationship is with Him.

But as for you, ye thought evil against me; but God meant it onto good, to bring to pass, as it is this day, to save many people alive.

— Genesis 50:20, kjv

Chapter XV

PERSEVERANCE

Perseverance means that all those who are truly born again will be kept by God's power and as Christians will persevere to the end of their lives. For scripture states that "being confident of this very thing, that He who hath begun a good work in you will perform it until the day of Jesus Christ." (Philippians 1:6, kjv) And if we have become united with Him in the likeness of death certainly we shall also be in the likeness of His resurrection. (Romans 6:5, kjv) But what is the guarantee that we will remain Christian until we die and that we will in fact live with God in heaven forever? Or at some time in life we will turn away from Christ and lose our salvation? As Christians we must remember that there is assurance that has been given that God's power will keep them as Christians until death and they will live with Christ in heaven forever. On the other hand scripture also makes it clear that continuing in the Christian life is evidence that a person is truly born again. The term "eternal security of the believer" is often used to describe the perseverance of the saints.

"For I come down from heaven, not to do mine own will but the will of him who sent me." And this is the Father's will who hath sent me, that of all that he hath given me I should lose nothing, but should raise it up in the last day. "And this is the will of him that sent me, that everyone who seeth the Son, and believeth on him, may have everlasting life; and I will raise him up at the last day" (John 38-40, kjv) Remember those given to the Son by the Father will not be lost. (John 6:39, kjv) Jesus says "my sheep hear my voice, and I know them, and they follow me, and I give them eternal life, and they shall never perish," and no one shall snatch them out of my hand. "My Father, who has given them to me, is greater than all, and no one is able to snatch them out of the Father's hand," (John 10:27-29, kjv)

This is not only "no one" but even ourselves can't move or take ourselves out of Christ's hand. This passage simply says we don't have the power to snatch ourselves out of his hands. If you could lose your salvation then it was not "eternal" in the first place. Eternal on the fact that is the opposite of death it is the opposite of judgment and separation from God. It is life that goes on forever in the presence of God. It would be unjust for God to give any kind of eternal punishment to those who are Christians. Because the word says there is "no condemnation" for them who are in Christ Jesus. (Romans 8:1, kjv) The soul that God places in us is evidence that is represented by and is the Holy Spirit within us and also God's "guarantee" that we will receive his promises. In the possession of our inheritance we are promised "in whom we also trusted, after ye heard the word of truth, the gospel of your salvation; in whom also after ye believed ye were sealed with that Holy Spirit of promise. "who is the earnest of our inheritance until the redemption of the purchased possession, unto the praise of his glory." (Ephesians 1:13-14, kjv) God's own faithfulness is pleaded to bring this about.

In I Perter 1:5, it states that we are

"kept by the power of God through faith unto salvation ready to be revealed in the last time." This can also mean "kept from escaping" and protected from attacks." God is protecting His believers from escaping his kingdom as well as protecting them from eternal attacks. God's power energizes and continually sustains individual personal faith. By not only guarding for our temporary goals but of the future full possession of all the blessings of our redemption. If God's guarding has its purpose for the preservation of believers until they receive their full, eternal salvation, then its safe to conclude that God will accomplish that purpose and they will attain that final salvation, then its safe to conclude that God will accomplish that purpose and they will attain that final salvation. God's power will continually work "through" their faith. Its all a matter of trust in God.

Remember God does not guard us apart from faith, but only working through our faith that we continue to believe in him. As Jesus says in John 8:31-32, "if you continue in my word, then are ye my disciples indeed; and ye shall know the trust and and the truth shall make you free." Continuing and living a life of obedience is the key. And of course "he whom endures until the end shall be saved." (Matthew 10:22, kjv) Faith is the one means of assurance that is named in the book of Hebrews. That those who fall away from fellowship with the church and from belief in Christ show that their faith was not real in the first place and that they were never part of the true body of Christ. It is clear in I John 2:19 "that they went out from us, but they were not of us, for if they had been of us, they would have continued with us; but they went out, that they might be made manifest that they were not of us".

The whole idea of perseverance is in listening to Jesus, doing as He says, and allowing him to transform your mind. (Romans 12:2, kjv) We need to stop trying and start trusting and He will lead you to a consistently Christian walk and set you free from your bondage to sin. John makes it clear in scripture that there are people in church who ave only an intellectual persuasion of the truth of the gospel but no genuine faith in there hearts. And scripture mentions in several places that unbelievers in fellowship with the visible church can give some external signs or indications that make them look like genuine believers. For instance, Judas, who betrayed Christ acted almost exactly as the other disciples for three years while walking with Jesus. They never recognized him but rather said, "Is it I?"

(Mark 14:19, Luke 22:23, John 13:22, kjv) Jesus knew who it was because He stated, "Did I not chose you, the twelve, and one of you is a devil?" (John 6:70, kjv) He knew from the beginning. (John 6:64, kjv) Paul states during his journey that he has been "in danger from false brethren," (II Corinthians 11:26, kjv) He also states that the servants of Satan "disguise themselves as servants of righteousness. (II Corinthians 11:15, kjv) This is not to say that all unbelievers in the church that give some sign of conversion are servants of Satan by undermining the work of the church but may be in the process of considering the claims of gospel and moving towards real faith. In many cases they be experiencing an inadequate explanation of the gospel message and therefore have not come to genuine conviction of the Holy Spirit. In an example given in the 4th chapter of the book of Mark, Jesus says "other seed fell on stony ground, where it had not much earth, and immediately it sprang up because it had no depth of earth. But when the sun was out it was scorched and because it had no root, it withered away. (Mark 4:5-6, kjv) Jesus Explains that some people when they hear the word, immediately they receive it with joy but they but they have no root in themselves, but endure for a while but when trials and tribulation come or persecution come on account of the word, they fall away. (Mark 4:16-17, kjv) This was an indication that there was no saving faith in their hearts only an appearance of conversion. They simply do not abide in Christ. (John 15:6, kjv) If we are not careful we could have our own witness compromised and our own lives influenced by those who we associate with. (Ephesians 5:7, kjv) And remember just because they have been associated with the Holy Spirit does not mean that influence was a redeeming work of the Holy Spirit in their lives, or that they were regenerated. (Hebrews 6:4-6, kjv) These are people no doubt have been affiliated closely with the fellowship of the church. They have tasted of the goodness of the word of God.

But in spite of all of this experience they commit apostasy and deliberately "crucify the Son of God afresh, and put Him to an open shame." (Hebrews 6:6, kjv) Then they are willingly rejecting these blessings and deciding against them. Then as scripture says it is impossible to restore them again to any kind of repentance or sorrow for sin. Believe it or not the Holy Spirit can serve to harden their hearts against conversion. In this case there is no perseverance. We will learn that depending on temporary blessings and experiences is not enough.

So what can give a believer genuine

assurance? First of all I must have present trust in Christ for salvation. Meaning continuing in the faith, grounded and settled and be not moved away from the hope of the gospel. (Colossians 1:23, kjv) We must "through faith and patient inherit the promise" (Hebrews 6:12, kjv) As a reminder John 3:16 may be translated who so ever is committed to, faith in, reliance upon or trust in shall not perish is not only a consent of the mind but an act of the heart and will. What about whats in our heart? Is there evidence of a regenerating work of the holy Spirit? There must be a subjective testimony of the Holy Spirit within our hearts bearing witness that we are God's children. (Romans 8:15-16, kjv, John 4:13, kjv) II Peter 1:10 says that we should add to our faith, virtue, knowledge, self-control, steadfastness, godliness and brotherly affection for assurance of no failure. "You will never fail" and confirm your call and election. The doctrine of the perseverance of the saints should be a tremendously comforting doctrine. No one having the assurance should doubt or say, "Will I be able to persevere in the end of my life and be saved?" A self examination should know that you will certainly persevere to the end by the power of the Holy Spirit working through your faith. (I Perter 1:5, kjv) "And this is the will of Him that sent me, that everyone who seeth the Son, and believeth on him, may have everlasting life; and I shall raise him up in the last day." (John 6:40, kjv)

Conclusion

I have tried to demonstrate in this book that the truth about a relationship has been misrepresented for a long time. Our society has suffered for a lack of knowledge about relationships. We have redefined relationship to fit our own desires and purposes and we have turned away from the truth as if it never existed. The results have not only affected our lives and our country but the world. As we can see, the major problem in our world is relationships. We can't get along with each other! While we struggle to make it right, we are simply getting further and further away from the truth.

We are trying to solve what really is

a much deeper problem than we would like to believe. I have attempted to reveal that the perception of men seems to be that a relationship is just another tool to exercise a form of selfish control or influence. There are ulterior motives for having a relationship with particular people in a particular way. I have exposed the fact that there simply are no teaching or positive guidelines of truth being used in most relationships. Only that which is created by society is said to be the right way to have a relationship.

No real concern has been considered of whether relationships are based on facts because of the ignorance about a relationship. As far as man is concerned, a relationship is based on however you perceive or pursue it. You just have to make it work or you can seek help from tested resources or ideas. Now we have relationships based on different recipes.

When all has been said it would seem like we would sooner or later question whether or not it makes sense to refer to the one who created relationships; Our Lord and Savior Jesus Christ, creator of the universe. He and He alone has provided us with everything we need to solve our relationship problems. As a matter of fact, the Bible is a book of relationships. The problem is we won't accept our problems as having anything to do with spirituality. Quite the contrary, that is exactly our problem and until we realize this our relationships are going to continue to fail and not be healed. The word of God can be depended upon to provide all of the necessary principles needed for a right relationship.

Joining is not something that we should take lightly with anything. There are questions that must be answered to our satisfaction. For instance why? what are the benefits? and is this the best for me?

The answers to these questions never seem to have an effect on our relationship to other people, only a personal choice. Since we can't see the whole picture the effect this choice has on our future, God has provided us a perception that is reliable to make the right decision about our joining in His word. But *"we must first seek ye the Kingdom of God and His righteousness and all these other things shall be added. (Matthew 6:33, kjv)* We are responsible for every decision we make and every association that affects our lives. And remember, what God has joined together is oneness with Him.

Bibliography of Helpful Resources

Bibles

1. The New Scofield Reference Bible C. I. Scofieid, D. D., Oxford University Press, Inc, 1967 KJV
2. The Nelson Study Bible Thomas Nelson Inc. 1997, Nashville TN, NKJV
3. The Greek New Testament Biblia –Druck Gmbh Struttgart, West Germany third Edition 1983
4. The NIV Thematic Reference Bible Zondervan Publishing House, 1984 International Bible Society

5. English Standard Version, 2000 Crossway Bible Ministry of good news publishing

Biblical Resource Tools

1. Dictionary of Paul and His Letters, Intervarsity Press, 1993
2. Dictionary of Biblical Imagery IVP Academic, Intervarsity Press 1998
3. Vine's Expository Dictionary of New Testament Words, Barbour and Company Inc. 1985
4. New Strong's Executive Concordance of the Bible, James Strong, L.L. S. T. D. Thomas Nelson Publish Publishers, 1990

Scriptural References

Chapter 1

Genesis 1:27, kjv
Psalms 8:58, kjv
Genesis 2:15-17, kjv
Genesis 3:8-10, kjv
John 17:21, kjv
Thessalonians 5:23 kjv
John 4:24 kjv
Genesis 1:28 kjv
Ephesians 1:4 kjv
Genesis 3:24 kjv
II Corinthians 6:14 kjv
Malachi 3:6 kjv
Romans 14:23 kjv
Jeremiah 50:5 kjv

II Corinthians 6:17 kjv
Ephesians 6:12 kjv
Isaiah 54:17 kjv

Chapter II

Genesis 2:18 kjv
Amos 3:3 kjv
I Corinthians 13:3-5 kjv
Psalms 51:5 kjv
Ephesians 2 kjv
Mark 10:19 kjv
Matthew 1:21 kjv
Matthew 11:28 kjv
Matthew 15:24 kjv
Luke 24:49 kjv
II Corinthians 6:14 kjv

Chapter III

I Corinthians 3:16-17 kjv
Ephesians 1:3 kjv
Romans 8:17 kjv
Romans 8:14 kjv

Ephesians 1:4 kjv
Ephesians 1:7 kjv
Matthew 20:28 kjv
Hebrew 9: kjv
Hebrew 2:8 kjv
Ephesians 1:11–12 kjv
Ephesians 1:13 kjv
Ephesians 1:21:–23, kjv

Chapter IV

Genesis 9:9–17 kjv
Genesis 15:18 kjv
Genesis 17:1–19 kjv
Exodus 24:1–8 kjv
Numbers 10:38 kjv
II Samuel 23:5 kjv
II Chronicles 13:5; 21:7 kjv
Jeremiah 31:31–34 kjv
Luke 22:20 kjv
Hebrew 8:8 9:15; 12:28 kjv
Hebrew 8:6; 12:24 kjv
I Corinthians 11:25 kjv

Genesis 21:27, 32 kjv

Joshua 9:11, 15 kjv

Exodus 34:10 kjv

Deuteronomy 4:23 kjv

Genesis 26:28-29, 31:50-52 kjv

Joshua 9:15-16 kjv

II Kings 17:41 kjv

Mark 2:14 kjv

Genesis 9:9-11 kjv

Ephesians 2:12 kjv

II Kings 11:17 kjv

II Chronicles 15:12 kjv

Nehemiah 10:29 kjv

Matthew 5:23-24 kjv

I Samuel 18:3, 23:18 kjv

I Samuel 20:8 kjv

Jeremiah 34:8 kjv

Joshua 9; kjv

Judges 2:2 kjv

Isaiah 28:15 kjv

Genesis 9:9, 17 kjv

Genesis 15:6 kjv

Exodus 9:4 kjv

Exodus 6:5-6 kjv

Exodus 24:3-8 kjv

Deuteronomy 5:2-3 kjv

Leviticus 20:9 kjv

I Kings 8:23 kjv

II Chronicles 6:14 kjv

Hebrew 1:5; 9:32 kjv

Proverbs 2:17 kjv

Psalms 25:10; 103:18 kjv

Jeremiah 33:19-26 kjv

Chapter V

Isaiah 21:4 kjv

II Kings 5:14 kjv

Leviticus 16:4, 24 kjv

John 1:6, 11 kjv

Matthew 3:11 kjv

Matthew 3:15 kjv

John 4:1-2 kjv

John 1:3 kjv

Acts 8:17 kjv

Acts 2:38 kjv

Romans 6:1-6 kjv

Acts 8:12-13, 36-38 kjv

Ephesians 4:5 kjv

John 14:26, 16:13 kjv

I Corinthians 6:11 kjv

Ephesians 4:30 kjv

Romans 3:23 kjv

Psalms 79:9, 85:4 51:12 kjv

Isaiah 25:6, 8-9 kjv

Isaiah 51:6 kjv

Psalms 36:10, 37:19-40 kjv

Luke 19:10 kjv

II Corinthians 5:19 kjv

Romans 5:9-10 kjv

Romans 2:13, 3:20 kjv

Romans 8:17 kjv

Revelation 21:1 kjv

Ephesians 2:8-9 kjv

Romans 3:28 kjv

Romans 3:20 kjv

Romans 6:12-13

Chapter VI

II Kings 22:2 kjv

II Kings 22:8 kjv

II Kings 22:11 kjv

Ecclesiastes 9:4 kjv

John 14:6 kjv

Jeremiah 50:55 kjv

Matthew 19:6 kjv

Acts 5:12-14 kjv

I Corinthians 10:17 kjv

I Corinthians 1:19 kjv

I Corinthians 1:20 kjv

Ephesians 4:16 kjv

Romans 12:9 kjv

Genesis 2:24 kjv

I Corinthians 16:17 kjv

Deuteronomy 6:4 kjv

Numbers 15:16 kjv

Mark 10:5 kjv

Zechariah 14:9 kjv

John 17:11 kjv

Chapter VII

Acts 13:10 kjv

Proverbs 14:12 kjv

II Corinthians 6:14 kjv

Proverbs 22:6 kjv

Amos 3:3 kjv

I Corinthians 12:1-7 kjv

Genesis 2:23 kjv

John 16:13 kjv

Luke 12:15b kjv

Genesis 2:17 kjv

Acts 17:28 kjv

Matthew 6:33 kjv

Chapter VIII

Acts 2:33 kjv

Luke 24:49 kjv

Acts 2:33, 38-39 kjv

Ephesians 1:13 kjv

Ephesians 1:4 kjv

Exodus 31:2-3 kjv

Judges 10, kjv

Judges 6:34 kjv
Judges 14:6, 19 kjv
I Samuel 10:6 kjv
Micah 3:8 kjv
Mark 1:10 kjv
Mark 13:11 kjv
Acts 2:1–47 kjv
Ephesians 1:14 kjv
I Corinthians 12:4-7 kjv
Romans 6:17-18 kjv
II Peter 1:4 kjv
Titus 1:4 kjv
II Corinthians 6:17-18 kjv

Chapter IX

Jeremiah 50:1–5 kjv
Isaiah 53:6 kjv
Jeremiah 50:6 kjv
Zechariah 11:4-5 kjv
Zechariah 11:5-6 kjv
Jeremiah 50:5 kjv
I Corinthians 1:10 kjv

Ephesians 4:16 kjv
Matthew 11:28 kjv
Ecclesiastes 9:4 kjv
Proverbs 11:21 kjv
Deuteronomy 6:10-12 kjv
Acts 4:12 kjv

Chapter X

Deuteronomy 6:4 kjv
Matthew 1:21 kjv
Ephesians 2:8, 9 kjv
Titus 3:5 kjv
Ephesians 1:6, 7 kjv
John 17:20:-22 kjv
Ephesians 1:5 kjv
I Thessalonians 5:9 kjv
I Thessalonians 4:16-17 kjv
Hebrews 4:12 kjv
I Corinthians 2:11 kjv
Job 32:8 kjv
Proverbs 20:27 kjv
I Corinthians 15:44 kjv

Chapter XI

Leviticus 26:16–39, kjv
Philippians 1:6, kjv
Matthew 17:3, kjv
Numbers 27:12–14, kjv
I Kings 11:11–14, kjv
I Kings 11:9–13, kjv
Job 5:17, kjv
Psalms 94:12, kjv
Psalms 94:10, kjv
Proverbs 26:3, kjv
Proverbs 22:15, kjv
Proverbs 29:17, kjv
Jeremiah 30:11, kjv
Isaiah 45:7, kjv
II Timothy 3:12, kjv
Hebrews 12:5, kjv
Hebrews 12:7, kjv

Chapter XII

Proverbs 22:15, kjv
Proverbs 10:13, kjv

Isaiah 53:5, kjv
Proverbs 13:24, kjv
Hebrews 12:5, kjv
Hebrews 12:11, kjv
Proverbs 3:11-12, kjv

Chapter XIII

Acts 24:2, kjv
Psalms 19:1, kjv
Psalms 104:19, 105:2, 6, kjv
Nehemiah 9:6-3 8, kjv
Matthews 6:25-34, kjv
Romans 8:28, kjv
Romans 8:18-25, kjv
Romans 8:29, kjv
Job 7:20, kjv
Psalms 36:6, kjv
Hebrews 9:27, kjv
II Chronicles 16:9, kjv
Psalms 84:11, kjv
I Corinthians 13:12, kjv
Psalms 77:19, kjv

Psalms 97:2, kjv

John 13:7, kjv

Psalms 73:13, kjv

Jeremiah 12:1, kjv

II Corinthians 4:17, kjv

II Corinthians 4:14-16, kjv

Galatians 6:9, kjv

CHAPTER XIV

Galatians 6:7, kjv

John 16:33, kjv

Ephesians 6:12, kjv

I Peter 5:7, kjv

Ephesians 1:4, kjv

Matthew 28:20, kjv

Matthew 11:29, kjv

Psalms 1:1-2, kjv

Proverbs 8:14, kjv

Isaiah 64:6, kjv

Proverbs 3:6, kjv

Romans 8:28, kjv

James 1:4, kjv

CHAPTER XV

Philippians 1:6, kjv
Romans 6:5, kjv
John 3 8-40, kjv
John 6:39, kjv
John 10:27-29, kjv
Romans 8:1, kjv
Ephesians 1:13-14, kjv
I Peter 1:5, kjv
John 8:31-32, kjv
Matthew 10:22, kjv
I John 2:19, kjv
Romans 12:2, kjv
Mark 14:19, kjv
Luke 22:23, kjv
John 13:22, kjv
John 6:70, kjv
John 6:64, kjv
II Corinthians 11:26, kjv
II Corinthians 11:15, kjv
Mark 4:5-6, kjv
Mark 4:16-17, kjv

John 15:6, kjv
Ephesians 5:7, kjv
Hebrews 6:4, kjv
Hebrews 6:6, kjv
Colossians 1:23
Hebrews 6:12
John 3:16
Romans 8:15–16
John 4:13
II Peter 1:10
I Peter 1:5
John 6:40

About the Author

Larry Adams is a native of Missouri, a child of God, a father, grandfather' Bible teacher, Biblical Counselor, husband and member of the body of Christ. His love for the Word of God has allowed him to express himself in writing to share his gift of the Word to the world. He has earned his BS. MS, Ed D from Lael University and Graduate School and has received certifications from Missouri Baptist College and Light University. He is a Board Certified Biblical Counselor and has been a bible teacher for over forty years. He is also a member of the International Board of Christians Counselors and the American Academy of Biblical Counselors.

Printed in the United States
by Baker & Taylor Publisher Services